The Holy Spirit Today

JOHN SIEBELING

johnsiebeling.com

JOHN SIEBELING

The Holy Spirit Today
Copyright © 2009 by John Siebeling

Request for information should be addressed to:

The Life Church, 1800 N. Germantown Parkway, Cordova, TN 38016

ISBN-10: 0-61528-968-1
ISBN-13: 978-0-61528-968-7

Printed in the United States of America.

johnsiebeling.com

CONTENTS

Dear friend,

Over the years, there have been a few significant teachings that have really changed my life. More than just sermons, I'm talking about powerful, transforming principles from God's Word. The role of the Holy Spirit, and specifically the baptism with the Holy Spirit, has been one of those life-changing teachings and experiences for me.

It's hard to believe that over 25 years ago I read a booklet much like this one and knelt beside my bed as a young man of 17 years and asked God to give me everything that He wanted to give me, including this gift of the Holy Spirit that I had just read about. That night changed my life and my prayer is that God would use this booklet to change your life.

John

John Siebeling

what do you think of
the Holy Spirit?

WHAT DO YOU THINK OF THE HOLY SPIRIT?

In order to understand the Holy Spirit and His role in our lives, we have to first make sure we have the right perspective. The best way to do this is by studying God's Word to find out what it has to say.

Acts 19:1-2 – *"While Apollos was at Corinth, Paul took the road through the interior and arrived at Ephesus. There he found some disciples and asked them, 'Did you receive the Holy Spirit when you believed?' They answered, 'No, we have not even heard that there is a Holy Spirit.'"*

We're going to explore this passage several times throughout this booklet because I think there are quite a few thoughts we can download from it about the Holy Spirit. Let's set the context - the Apostle

Paul is traveling, planting churches, and just as he arrives in Ephesus he runs into some disciples. These "disciples" were Christian believers, and I think it's pretty significant that the first question Paul asks them is about the Holy Spirit. I believe this shows the importance of the Holy Spirit, and their answer is really interesting. They said they had *"not even heard that there is a Holy Spirit."* I think we're in a similar situation today. Many believers don't have a solid Biblical foundation about the Holy Spirit.

In fact, as I've talked to different Christians about the Holy Spirit, many are uninformed; they've never been taught about the Holy Spirit. Others are misinformed, having been taught inaccurate, non-Biblical things about the Holy Spirit. Some have been told the Holy Spirit isn't for today or even that it is of the devil.

The reason I called the booklet "The Holy Spirit Today" is because the Holy Spirit is for today. We need Him in our lives today and He is working in the church around the world today! Still, other believers are apprehensive, maybe even fearful, not fully understanding the work and the power of the Holy Spirit, so they tend to shrink back. Finally, there's a whole segment of the church that is indifferent, lacking a real hunger for God.

I really believe God has an incredible plan for your life and a part of that great plan is understanding and receiving the life, power, freedom and strength that the Holy Spirit can bring.

In the Bible, Jesus used this expression frequently: *"The kingdom of heaven is like..."* He was constantly trying to help the people of His time (and ours) understand how God thinks and operates. Obviously, God's thoughts are on a completely different plane than our thoughts...

Isaiah 55:8-11 – *"This plan of mine is not what you would work out, neither are my thoughts the same as yours! For just as the heavens are higher than the earth, so are my ways higher than yours, and my thoughts than yours. As the rain and snow come down from heaven and stay upon the ground to water the earth, and cause the grain to grow and to produce seed for the farmer and bread for the hungry, so also is my Word. I send it out, and it always produces fruit. It shall accomplish all I want it to and prosper everywhere I send it."* (TLB)

Simply put, our lives as believers are spent renewing our minds so we can think like God thinks, which enables us to walk according to God's principles. When we do this, not only will we experience fulfillment deep within but we'll also see God's blessings poured into our lives. Ultimately those blessings will overflow to those around us.

The role of the Holy Spirit, and specifically the baptism with the Holy Spirit, is a subject that requires us to think the way God thinks. For me, this spiritual concept was not as challenging as it may be for some other Christians. From the very beginning of my walk with Jesus I was surrounded by people who not only understood the power of being filled with the Holy Spirit, but also believed that this spiritual gift was for every single person who wanted it. I'm proud of my

Spirit-filled heritage and the foundation it has been in
my life ever since I was a teenager.

However, I'm also aware
that clear, sound
Biblical teaching on
this subject has often
been set aside and
replaced with an
encouragement
to simply

"If we want to receive
all God has for us, then
we're going to have to
move beyond the natural
realm into the
supernatural realm."

"believe and receive. If God wants you to have it, then
it will just happen." I've even heard good-hearted
spiritual leaders encouraging people to "bypass their
mind" in order to receive the Holy Spirit because they
could never comprehend the greatness of this gift from
God. While this sounds spiritual, it's really not true.

Our ability to believe, which is called faith, increases when we hear the Word (Romans 10:17)...and not just hear but also understand. The Apostle Paul wrote in Ephesians 3:18 that he was praying for the Ephesians to be able to comprehend God's love and all that was found within that love. I don't think he would have prayed for them to comprehend His love if it wasn't a possibility. The reason he prayed was because he knew comprehension wouldn't come through natural means, but only through supernatural, spiritual means.

If we want to receive all God has for us, then we're going to have to move beyond the natural realm into the supernatural realm. That's not scary, weird or spooky, and it's not "bypassing your mind." It simply means being open to all God has for us and making a commitment to believe and live according to the supernatural realm described in God's Word, instead of living as a Christian guided by the natural realm.

I Corinthians 2:14-15 – *"But the natural, nonspiritual man does not accept or welcome or admit into his heart the gifts and teachings and revelations of the Spirit of God, for they are folly (meaningless nonsense) to him; and he is incapable of knowing them [of progressively recognizing, understanding, and becoming better acquainted with them] because they are spiritually discerned and estimated and appreciated. But the spiritual man tries all things [he examines, investigates, inquires into, questions, and discerns all things]..."* (AMP)

It's easy to be open to the teachings we like, or that make us feel good, or correspond to how we've been

raised. But it's not so easy to take in the teachings
that correct us or challenge our thoughts and
mindsets, or even our theology. According to this
passage, natural non-
spiritual Christians
do not accept the
gifts and teachings
and revelations of
the Spirit of God.
They look at these
things as foolish and
dismiss them as meaningless. But, it says
the spiritual person examines, investigates, inquires
and looks into all that God has promised in His Word.
Then after looking into it, this kind of Christian opens
the door of his or her heart and receives these gifts
and teachings of the Spirit. As a result, their life will

"It simply means
being open to all
God has for us..."

continually change and improve; they'll be transformed into God's image. We need to always make sure we are the kind of Christians who have open hearts and minds, ready to receive the teachings of the Word.

There are very clear instructions in God's Word that can help us not only receive this great gift of the Holy Spirit, but also walk in this blessing and see it developed in our lives. God's Word is the key and everything in our lives should spring from it. Remember what it says in Isaiah 55: God's Word goes out and is alive, and powerful, and effective. The Bible says when it goes forth, it accomplishes His purposes and doesn't return void; therefore, we'll see it produce results in our lives.

Who is the Holy Spirit?

WHO IS THE HOLY SPIRIT?

Here are three simple points to describe who the Holy Spirit is. They might seem a little elementary, but they can help us to understand more about the Holy Spirit.

1. The Holy Spirit is a person.

This one comes as a surprise to many people. The King James Version of the Bible uses the name Holy Ghost, and maybe this is the word that trips up some people...they picture Casper the Friendly Ghost with a holy aura or something. However, just like Jesus, who is fully God and fully man, the Holy Spirit is fully God but also functions as a person.

How do we know? Think about three of the qualities and characteristics you and I have as people. We have a mind; we can think. We have emotion; we can feel.

We also have a will; we can choose. The Holy Spirit has these three qualities as well.

Romans 8:27 tells us the Holy Spirit has a mind: *"And he who searches our hearts knows the **mind** of the Spirit..."*

Ephesians 4:30 shows us He has emotions: *"And do not **grieve** the Holy Spirit of God, with whom you were sealed for the day of redemption."*

And I Corinthians 12:11 talks about His will: *"But one and the same Spirit works all these things, distributing to each one individually as He **wills**."* (NASB)

2. The Holy Spirit is God.

The Holy Spirit is not part-God, but fully God. We believe there is one God, eternally existing in three persons: Father, Son (Jesus Christ) and Holy Spirit. These three are co-equal. Our God is a triune God, meaning three in one.

Now, let's take these first two statements, bring them together and add one final thought...

3. The Holy Spirit is the person of God in the now.

In other words, when the Holy Spirit was poured out in Acts 2 (we'll study about this later), He came to live within us. This is important because before this outpouring, the Holy Spirit only moved **upon** certain chosen men; it was impossible for the holiness and the purity of God to dwell inside a person who was not born again and not set free of his or her sin nature. But once Jesus died on the cross for our sins and rose again on the third day with complete victory over sin and death, He then ascended into Heaven so that now the Holy Spirit could come down and dwell **within** all men.

Jesus actually told His disciples it was to their advantage that He was going away because only then could the Holy Spirit come and occupy the hearts of all men:

"The Holy Spirit is not part-God, but fully God."

"However, I am telling you nothing but the truth when I say it is profitable

(good, expedient, advantageous) for you that I go away.
Because if I do not go away, the Comforter (Counselor,
Helper, Advocate, Intercessor, Strengthener, Standby)
will not come to you [into close fellowship with you];
but if I go away, I will send Him to you [to be in close
fellowship with you]." -

John 16:7 (AMP)

The Holy Spirit is the one who convicts us and encourages us. When we say we sense God's presence, we are sensing the presence of the Holy Spirit. The great news is, He is strengthening, comforting, and leading us every moment of our

"He is the person of God in the now, and He lives inside of us."

lives! He is the person of God in the now, and He lives inside of us! I Corinthians 3:16 says, *"Don't you know that you yourselves are God's temple and that God's Spirit lives in you?"*

what is the baptism
with the Holy Spirit?

WHAT IS THE BAPTISM WITH THE HOLY SPIRIT?

Now that we've talked about who the Holy Spirit is and some of the ways He impacts our lives, let's talk specifically about the baptism with the Holy Spirit. Many people wonder where the expression "baptized with the Holy Spirit" comes from. Jesus was the first one to say it, and His words are recorded in the Book of Acts, chapter 1.

Jesus had died on the cross, been risen from the dead, and had just spent many days ministering to His disciples. Then, as He was preparing to ascend into heaven, one of the last things He instructed His followers to do was to wait in Jerusalem for the gift that His Father promised. He then said, *"...which you have heard me speak about. For John baptized with water, but in a few days you will be **baptized with the***

Holy Spirit." (Acts 1:4-5) He was referring to what He
had told them during the Last Supper, several hours
before He was arrested.

Jesus knew He was on His way up to heaven, and that
the Holy Spirit was on His way down to earth. But
the disciples had grown used to having Jesus with
them, and when He started talking about leaving, they
became concerned and anxious. So, to get them ready,
Jesus spent quite a bit of time in the last months of
His life teaching the disciples about the Holy Spirit.

In John 14:15-18, He told The Twelve: *"If you love
Me, keep My commandments. And I will pray the
Father, and He will give you another Helper, that He
may abide with you forever— the Spirit of truth, whom
the world cannot receive, because it neither sees Him*

nor knows Him; but you know Him, for He dwells with
you and will be in you. I will not leave you orphans; I
will come to you." (NKJV)

I would encourage you to take some time and read
through John, the fourth book of the New Testament,
chapters 14-17 to learn more about what Jesus said
about the Holy Spirit. Reading them will encourage
you to pursue a relationship with the Holy Spirit as a
part of your everyday life.

Let's put a definition to this term, *"baptized with the*
Holy Spirit."

The word baptize essentially means "to immerse."
Holy Spirit baptism is an infilling experience that
takes place when we open our lives to God without

reservation, and we ask Him to baptize (immerse) us with His Holy Spirit. This incredible experience will catapult you into a new level in your walk with God and you'll begin to see results in the natural as well as the spiritual. When we are baptized with the Holy Spirit, our spirits become sensitized to the spirit realm and what God is doing in it.

"This incredible experience will catapult you into a new level..."

In the book of Acts there are several stories of people receiving the baptism with the Holy Spirit, and in these accounts some common factors are present. Let's read through these verses and draw some important conclusions.

Acts 2:1-21, 37-39 - Pentecost: The Initial Outpouring

When the day of Pentecost came, they were all together in one place. Suddenly a sound like the blowing of a violent wind came from heaven and filled the whole house where they were sitting. They saw what seemed to be tongues of fire that separated and came to rest on each of them.

Now there were staying in Jerusalem God-fearing Jews from every nation under heaven. When they heard this sound, a crowd came together in bewilderment, because each one heard them speaking in his own language. Utterly amazed, they asked: "Are not all these men who are speaking Galileans? Then how is it that each of us hears them in his own native language? Parthians, Medes and Elamites; residents of Mesopotamia, Judea and Cappadocia, Pontus and

Asia, Phrygia and Pamphylia, Egypt and the parts of Libya near Cyrene; visitors from Rome (both Jews and converts to Judaism); Cretans and Arabs-we hear them declaring the wonders of God in our own tongues!" Amazed and perplexed, they asked one another, "What does this mean?" Some, however, made fun of them and said, "They have had too much wine." Then Peter stood up with the Eleven, raised his voice and addressed the crowd: "Fellow Jews and all of you who live in Jerusalem, let me explain this to you; listen carefully to what I say. These men are not drunk, as you suppose. It's only nine in the morning! No, this is what was spoken by the prophet Joel: 'In the last days, God says, I will pour out my Spirit on all people. Your sons and daughters will prophesy, your young men will see visions, your old men will dream dreams. Even on my servants, both men and women, I will pour out my Spirit in those days, and they will prophesy. I will show wonders in the heaven above and signs on the earth below, blood and fire and billows of smoke. The sun will be turned to darkness and the moon to blood before the coming of the great and glorious day of the Lord. And everyone who calls on the name of the Lord will be saved.'"

When the people heard this, they were cut to the heart and said to Peter and the other apostles, "Brothers, what shall we do?" Peter replied, "Repent and be baptized, every one of you, in the name of Jesus Christ for the forgiveness of your sins. And you will receive the gift of the Holy Spirit. The promise is for you and your children and for all who are far off - for all whom the Lord our God will call."

Acts 8:4-8, 14-17 - Revival in Samaria

Those who had been scattered preached the word wherever they went. Philip went down to a city in Samaria and proclaimed the Christ there. When the crowds heard Philip and saw the miraculous signs he did, they all paid close attention to what he said. With shrieks, evil spirits came out of many, and many paralytics and cripples were healed. So there was great joy in that city.

When the apostles in Jerusalem heard that Samaria had accepted the word of God, they sent Peter and John to them. When they arrived, they prayed for them that they might receive the Holy Spirit, because the Holy Spirit had not yet come upon any of them; they had simply been baptized into the name of the Lord Jesus. Then Peter and John placed their hands on them, and they received the Holy Spirit.

Acts 10:44-48 - At the house of Cornelius

While Peter was still speaking these words, the Holy Spirit came on all who heard the message. The circumcised believers who had come with Peter were astonished that the gift of the Holy Spirit had been poured out even on the Gentiles. For they heard them speaking in tongues and praising God. Then Peter said, "Can anyone keep these people from being baptized with water? They have received the Holy Spirit just as we have." So he ordered that they be baptized in the name of Jesus Christ. Then they asked Peter to stay with them for a few days.

Acts 19:1-7- In the City of Ephesus

While Apollos was at Corinth, Paul took the road through the interior and arrived at Ephesus. There he found some disciples and asked them, "Did you receive the Holy Spirit when you believed?" They answered, "No, we have not even heard that there is a Holy Spirit." So Paul asked, "Then what baptism did you receive?" "John's baptism," they replied. Paul said, "John's baptism was a baptism of repentance. He told the people to believe in the one coming after him, that is, in Jesus." On hearing this, they were baptized into the name of the Lord Jesus. When Paul placed his hands on them, the Holy Spirit came on them, and they spoke in tongues and prophesied. There were about twelve men in all.

In reading these excerpts from the Book of Acts, I have found there are vital truths that are threaded through them all, but there are six things we need to know about the baptism with the the Holy Spirit.

Six things you need to know:

1. There was an overwhelming inbreaking of God's presence felt by all.

Notice a few of the key words from the passages we just read in Acts: suddenly... sound... saw... fell... heard... In other words, something BIG was happening, and it was obvious to each person who was there. This is really an important point: God's presence can be felt and experienced. Earlier we focused on what distinguishes the Holy Spirit as a person, and we saw that the Holy Spirit has a mind, will and emotions. The Bible says we are created in the image of God (Genesis 1:27), so we are given these same abilities. We understand what it's like to feel joy and sorrow, pain and freedom. The truth is, God experiences all of these things and He has made us to feel them and experience them as well. In fact, this is a part of how we relate to God.

David wrote in Psalm 16:11, *"You have made known to me the path of life; you will fill me with joy in your presence, with eternal pleasures at your right hand."*

Think about what David is saying: when we sense God's presence, when He leads us and gives us direction, there is nothing like it. The joy we experience is amazing! Think about a time when you really sensed God's love or His leading in your life. You could hardly contain yourself! It's an amazing thing that we can actually experience the presence of God.

We were made to experience God's presence. I know there are some who would caution you against emotionalism, and in reference to your growth as a Christian, that is a good point. However, there is nothing wrong with feeling and expressing emotion as a part of your relationship with God. In the dictionary, emotionalism is defined as the tendency to place too much value on emotion. This is the extreme, and emotionalism is something we should stay away from. But to avoid emotionalism doesn't mean you must avoid all emotion.

I'm not sure where the idea came from that in your relationship with God you must set your emotions aside. In truth, that's an extreme approach and should be avoided as well. Just as we shouldn't focus solely on an emotional relationship with God, we also shouldn't focus purely on an intellectual relationship with God. Balance is always the key. We were made in

God's image and we relate to Him with all that we are. Jesus said in Mark 12:30, *"Love the Lord your God with all your heart and with all your soul and with all your mind and with all your strength."* Your emotions are a part of your soul realm so, as you can see, we're instructed to love Him and serve Him and relate to Him with all that we are, including our emotions!

The Apostle Paul spent a lot of time in the book of I Corinthians dealing with these issues. Apparently, the Christians who went to the church in Corinth were having trouble finding a balance in living out the Spirit-filled life. They were so excited about operating in the gifts of the Spirit, they were letting their emotions take over and were getting carried away. So Paul wrote many suggestions, but I think this one is important and sums up how to maintain balance.

He wrote in I Corinthians 14:32-33, *"The spirits of prophets are subject to the control of prophets. For God is not a God of disorder but of peace."* In other words, when the Christian is operating in a spiritual gift the person is the one in control, not the gift.

His point is we don't lose conscious control when God is moving in our life. We're responsible for keeping our spirit under control. We know that God's nature is orderly and controlled. God is not into disorder and confusion or any type of overly emotional or "weird" behavior. When I teach on the Holy Spirit, I spend a lot of time and effort trying to take the "weird" out of the equation for people. Operating in the Holy Spirit is not a "Twilight Zone" type of experience. It's not dark and scary. And how could it be? God is full of life and light; He is peaceful, stable, and consistent.

2. The baptism with the Holy Spirit is an experience separate from salvation, although it can occur simultaneously.

As we begin to explore this conclusion, let me make it really clear that when we become Christians, we receive the Holy Spirit. The Bible tells us in I Corinthians 12:3 - *"...no one can say, 'Jesus is Lord,' except by the Holy Spirit."* One of the important roles of the Holy Spirit is to draw us to Christ and to lead us into relationship with Him. When we ask God to forgive us of our sins and invite Christ into our heart, the Holy Spirit is involved all the way! So, just to be really clear: as Christians, we have the Holy Spirit living inside of us. Therefore, the baptism with the Holy Spirit is a separate experience since we receive the Holy Spirit at salvation.

Let's take a look at Jesus and His disciples. After Jesus had endured the suffering of the cross, He was raised from the dead. The Bible tells us that for forty days after His resurrection He showed Himself to His disciples and gave many convincing proofs that He was alive (Acts 1:3). Let's look at two of the times when Jesus met with His disciples after He was raised from the dead.

Resurrection Day

If you read John 20 you will get a better picture of this entire day, but I'm sure it was a wild one for the disciples. Rumors were flying about what had happened to Jesus' missing body, and as the disciples gathered behind a locked door—in fear for their lives—Jesus appeared to them. He showed them His hands and His side to prove it was Him. They were filled with joy. Then, Jesus did something unusual...

*"And with that he breathed on them and said, **'Receive the Holy Spirit.'"** –* John 20:22

Theologically, I think this experience represents the born again experience for the disciples, and as we see, they received the Holy Spirit. The ultimate price had been paid: Jesus had conquered death, hell and the grave. Without a doubt, it was a powerful moment in their lives.

Ascension Day

Then, before He ascends into Heaven, He gives them another strong encouragement...

Acts 1:4-9 – *On one occasion, while he was eating with them, he gave them this command: "Do not leave Jerusalem, but wait for the gift my Father promised, which you have heard me speak about. For John baptized with water, but in a few days you will be baptized with the Holy Spirit." So when they met together, they asked him, "Lord, are you at this time going to restore the kingdom to Israel?" He said to them: "It is not for you to know the times or dates the Father has set by his own authority. But you will receive power when the Holy Spirit comes on you; and you will be my witnesses in Jerusalem, and in all Judea and Samaria, and to the ends of the earth." After he said this, he was taken up before their very eyes, and a cloud hid him from their sight.*

We know Jesus is giving them this encouragement after He had breathed on them and said, *"Receive the Holy Spirit."* So, obviously he is talking about something different than just the act of receiving the Holy Spirit that comes with the born again experience. It is a second experience He's referring to, and Jesus uses a new expression to describe it: *"baptized with the Holy Spirit."* In fact, He gives them the commission to reach Jerusalem, Judea and Samaria, and the ends of the earth. But, first, they need to be baptized with the Holy Spirit and receive the power needed to do the job! This is actually one of the greatest aspects of the Holy Spirit for us today. **The Holy Spirit gives us the power we need for daily living and the things that God has called us to do!**

Acts 2 records this second experience. As the disciples were waiting and praying, the Holy Spirit descended upon them and they were baptized with the Holy Spirit.

In the other passages from Acts that we read earlier, the same idea of a second experience exists. In Acts 8, when Philip went to preach in Samaria, great revival broke out. The Apostles in Jerusalem heard about what was happening so Peter and John went to see for themselves. Notice, their first order of business was to make sure the new converts were filled with the Holy Spirit:

Acts 8:14-17 – *"When the apostles in Jerusalem heard that Samaria had accepted the word of God, they sent Peter and John to them. When they arrived,*

they prayed for them that they might receive the Holy
Spirit, because the Holy Spirit had not yet come upon
any of them; they had simply been baptized into the
name of the Lord Jesus. Then Peter and John placed
their hands on them, and they received the Holy
Spirit."

The same approach is found in Acts 19. As the
Apostle Paul entered the city of Ephesus, he met
twelve "disciples" who had been baptized into
John's baptism. The first thing he wanted to know is
if they had received the Holy Spirit. Listen to their
response, "No, we have not even heard that there is
a Holy Spirit." I think this response is a very common
one heard throughout the Church today. While most
Christians have heard of the Holy Spirit, many haven't
heard a lot about the baptism with the Holy Spirit.

In my experience, I have found so many churches today that teach very little on the work of the Holy Spirit. When we really teach a sound, balanced message about all aspects of the Holy Spirit straight from the Bible, blinders fall from people's eyes and they can open their hearts and receive all that God has for them.

3. Speaking in other tongues is an indicator of Holy Spirit baptism.

In nearly every passage we read in the book of Acts concerning the activity of the Holy Spirit, we usually find the phrase "speaking or praying in other tongues."

Acts 2:4 – *"All of them were filled with the Holy Spirit and began to **speak in other tongues**..."*

Acts 10:44-46 – *"While Peter was still speaking these words, the Holy Spirit fell upon all those who heard the word. And those of the circumcision who believed were astonished, as many as came with Peter, because **the gift of the Holy Spirit** had been poured out on the Gentiles also. **For they heard them speak with tongues and magnify God."** (NKJV)

Acts 19:6 – *"And when Paul had laid his hands on them, the Holy Spirit came upon them, and **they spoke with tongues** and prophesied."* (NKJV)

The act of speaking in other tongues is *your* response to being baptized with the Holy Spirit. The Holy Spirit will by no means take control of you and force you to speak in a foreign language. Let's take a look at a passage to see how Jesus described it.

John 7:37-39 – *"On the last and greatest day of the Feast, Jesus stood and said in a loud voice, 'If anyone is thirsty, let him come to me and drink. Whoever believes in me, as the Scripture has said, streams of living water will flow from within him.' By this he meant the Spirit, whom those who believed in him were later to receive."*

When we open our hearts and pray in faith that God would baptize us with the Holy Spirit, it's like a river begins to flow on the inside of us. If we allow God to have His way, that living water will flow right up and overflow into an awesome new prayer language. We'll describe the benefits to this new prayer language later, but know that it's a powerful experience and one you don't want to miss out on! It's God's gift to us, and not something we have to shrink back from or be afraid of.

The thing about a gift is, in order for it to be enjoyed, it has to be given and it has to be received. What if you got a note in the mail telling you someone had given you a million dollars, and all you had to do in order to get it was come down to the bank, show your ID, and sign some papers? I don't know about you, but I think I'd drop everything and go check it out. But until I go and do my part, the gift just sits there on the shelf. It's the same way with gifts from God; He freely gives the gift, but you have to receive it. And it's an awesome gift – ours for the asking and receiving!

Luke 11:11-13 – *"Which of you fathers, if your son asks for a fish, will give him a snake instead? Or if he asks for an egg, will give him a scorpion? If you then, though you are evil, know how to give good gifts to your children, how much more will your Father in heaven give the Holy Spirit to those who ask him!"*

Remember, we're talking about the **gift** of the Holy Spirit. It's an amazing gift that will forever change your life. With that gift comes an incredible ability to pray in a different language. This is a special language God gives to enable you to communicate directly with Him in a special way. It's given for the benefit of the believer, to "super-charge" your life and relationship with God.

Paul encourages us in I Corinthians 14:1 to *"...eagerly desire spiritual gifts..."* As we open our lives to God and believe Him for all the great things He has for us, a new desire to understand and flow in spiritual gifts will rise up on the inside.

4. The laying on of hands can be helpful, but isn't essential.

When I refer to "laying on of hands," picture someone praying for you and putting their hand on your shoulder. In Acts 8:14-17, the Apostles showed up, laid hands on everyone, and everyone they touched received the Holy Spirit. But in Acts 10:44-46 Peter was preaching, and no one was laying hands on anyone, yet the Holy Spirit "fell" and they were all filled with the Holy Spirit. Sometimes it makes a difference when you have people around encouraging you and laying hands on you. There are times in our church services when we pray for people and we lay hands on them, but the truth is it isn't absolutely necessary. God can literally do anything He wants to do. The Bible does encourage us to agree in prayer

with one another, and we shouldn't resist having
people pray for us or shy away from it, but we don't
have to be limited by it either.

I told the story in the introduction of this book about
how I received the Holy Spirit: kneeling beside my
bed. It was just me and the Holy Spirit. I've included
a simple prayer at the end of this booklet, and the
great thing is that you can pray right now and receive.
There's nothing else you have to do. All you have to do
is ask God.

5. Holy Spirit baptism was a normal and expected experience in the New Testament.

Again, in Acts 8:14-17, when the Apostles showed up
in Samaria, the first order of business was ensuring

everyone had received the Holy Spirit. We see the
same thing in Acts 19. The first question Paul asked,
"Did you receive the Holy Spirit when you believed?"

There wasn't much debate about it then; it was simply
the natural next step. It's only now, thousands of years
later, that there are all sorts of different viewpoints
and controversies about this subject. Over the years
I have watched hundreds of believers understand
and receive the Holy Spirit simply because I opened
the Bible and showed them the Scriptures. It's hard
to deny once you read the Word with an open heart.
More than ever, I see a genuine excitement about this
subject as people's hearts are open to all that God has
for them.

On the day of Pentecost, when Peter stood up and addressed the crowd, He wisely referenced an Old Testament prophecy predicting the day when God would pour out the Holy Spirit…

"…being baptized with the Holy Spirit is an experience we all can receive."

Joel 2:28-29 – *"And afterward, I will pour out my Spirit on all people. Your sons and daughters will prophesy, your old men will dream dreams, your young men will see visions. Even on my servants, both men and women, I will pour out my Spirit in those days."*

This was an amazing word the prophet Joel gave in his day, because in the Old Testament, the Holy Spirit moved mightily **upon** certain chosen men and women. But Joel spoke of a time in the future when the Holy Spirit would **dwell** mightily **within** all men and women who seek after Him. That time came on the day of Pentecost in Acts 2, and we're still living in that season of promise.

6. The experience is for everyone!

This is my favorite point of all the six because I know beyond a shadow of a doubt this is not an exclusive gift. The experience of being baptized with the Holy Spirit is an experience we all can receive. It's not just for some of us. There are some who believe you're not filled with the Holy Spirit unless you speak with tongues, while another group would suggest we could all be filled with the Holy Spirit, but we might not all be able to speak in tongues. The second group believes that it is a gift from God, but it's not for everyone. Usually, they draw this opinion from a series of rhetorical questions that Paul asks at the end of 1 Corinthians 14.

Let's focus on this for a minute. **I think it's important to know that God has promised this great gift of a personal prayer language to every single one of us.** It's worth taking some time to draw a clear distinction between what I call the *public gift of tongues* and the *private gift* (personal prayer language). In I Corinthians chapters 12 through 14 the Apostle Paul addresses the subject of the gifts of the Holy Spirit. There are nine specific gifts listed and the last two are *"the* gift of speaking in other tongues" and "the gift of interpretation of tongues." These two gifts work in tandem and must accompany one another when expressed in a corporate setting.

There are two important things we need to understand about the nine gifts of the Spirit:

1. They are designed for the building up of the corporate body.

2. They are given by the Holy Spirit as He determines.

As we see from scripture, we don't possess the gifts, the Holy Spirit does. He just gives them to us as He determines, when He determines, for the purpose of the church body. What the disciples experienced on the day of Pentecost was not this public gift of speaking in other tongues. Rather, it was a personal gift, what many call a personal prayer language. This is different from the public gift of tongues because it isn't used to help the corporate church body - it's literally a gift from God for you! It's a prayer language that God gives you for your benefit. A little later we'll look at the benefits of praying in other tongues.

Take a minute and look at these three verses and let's tie a few words together.

Acts 1:4-5 – *"On one occasion, while he was eating with them, he gave them this command: 'Do not leave Jerusalem, but wait for **the gift** my Father **promised**, which you have heard me speak about. For John*

baptized with water, but in a few days you will be
baptized with the Holy Spirit.'"

Acts 2:38-39 – *"Then Peter said to them, 'Repent,*
and let every one of you be baptized in the name of
Jesus Christ for the remission of sins; and you shall
*receive the **gift of the Holy Spirit**. For **the promise** is to*
you and to your children, and to all who are afar off, as
many as the Lord our God will call.'" (NKJV)

Acts 10:44-46 – *"While Peter was still speaking these*
words, the Holy Spirit fell upon all those who heard
the word. And those of the circumcision who believed
were astonished, as many as came with Peter, because
*the **gift of the Holy Spirit** had been poured out on the*
Gentiles also. For they heard them speak with tongues
and magnify God." (NKJV)

When Jesus was giving His final words before He
ascended, He referred to the outpouring of the Holy
Spirit in two unique ways:

1. Jesus told them they were about to receive **the gift**
that His Father had talked about.

2. Jesus said it was **a promise**. Jesus is specifically
referring to what the disciples experienced in
Acts 2. Go back and read it again. It was an amazing
experience then, just as it is today.

After this fantastic experience, Peter stands up to
give some explanation and he uses the exact same
language. He speaks about **the gift** and **the promise**.
There's something important about Peter's words.
Jesus promised the disciples. Peter promises the

crowd standing before him, and he also extends the promise of the baptism with the Holy Spirit to their children, and to all who are afar off, "and as many as the Lord our God will call."

That last phrase refers specifically to you and me. We're a part of the many that the Lord our God has called! **It's important for us to know that God hasn't just chosen us and saved us, but He's also called us!** Check out this great verse:

Romans 8:30 – *"And having chosen us, he called us to come to him; and when we came, he declared us 'not guilty,' filled us with Christ's goodness, gave us right standing with himself, and promised us his glory."* (TLB)

The gift of the
Holy Spirit.

THE GIFT OF THE HOLY SPIRIT.

1. When you pray in tongues you're walking in obedience to God's Word.

Ephesians 5:18-19 – *"Do not get drunk on wine, which leads to debauchery. Instead, be filled with the Spirit."*

I love this command from the Bible. I think sometimes people see being baptized with the Holy Spirit as a suggestion or an option, but the Apostle Paul is really commanding us right here in this passage to be filled! Paul also writes these words in I Corinthians 14:18, *"I thank God that I speak in tongues more than all of you."* Obviously, this gift and his commitment to it were a huge part of his life.

In essence, all the promises and encouragements we've focused on in the first part of this booklet are ours when we fully obey God's Word. Great benefits flow into our lives when we obey God's Word. Don't be deceived and think you have to fully understand something before you can be obedient. Many times we don't have a full picture, but we're invited by God to move forward. That's really where the blessing lies: God sees we trust Him, and He keeps leading and rewarding us.

2. When you pray in tongues, it builds you up on the inside.

I Corinthians 14:4 – *"He who speaks in a tongue edifies himself..."*

When you look up the word "edify" in the Strong's Greek Dictionary it says - to be a house builder, i.e. construct or (figuratively) confirm. That's a great way to say it. The Holy Spirit is like a spiritual house builder. When we pray in tongues, we're building up our inner man. There is a "God confidence" that rises up on the inside. As we walk through each day, there are always quite a few opportunities to get negative or fearful or critical. We all face obstacles. We need God's strength and confidence rooted deep down on the inside. This great gift from God enables us to walk in an inner strength that we need to emerge victoriously on the other side of challenges we face – not to just make it through them, but to possess the victory!

3. When you pray in tongues, it releases faith into your heart.

Jude 20 – *"But you, dear friends, build yourselves up in your most holy faith and pray in the Holy Spirit."*

This is similar to being built up on the inside, but you could look at it like this: when you're built up on the inside, it will give you the confidence you need to step out in faith. Someone once said that faith is the currency in the Kingdom of God. I think this is the perfect way to describe how

"There is a God Confidence that rises up on the inside."

important faith is in our lives. We need faith to move forward and take possession of the things God has promised us! Here's just how important faith is to God:

Hebrews 11:6 – *"And without faith it is impossible to please God, because anyone who comes to him must believe that he exists and that he rewards those who earnestly seek him."*

So, if faith comes when I pray in tongues and I need faith to please God, thank God for the gift of the baptism with the Holy Spirit, which releases faith into my heart!

4. When you pray in tongues, you're praying and walking in God's power.

Acts 1:8 – *"But you will receive power when the Holy Spirit comes on you; and you will be my witnesses in Jerusalem, and in all Judea and Samaria, and to the ends of the earth."*

Jesus didn't want His disciples going out to fulfill the great commission He had given them until they had the power they needed to fulfill the task. In fact, in Luke 24:49 He told the disciples they needed to *"stay in the city until you have been clothed with power from on high."* That's how important it was to Him. Jesus knew they would need God's power if they were going to accomplish God's assignments. The same is true for us. God's given us some great things to do, and we're going to need His power to accomplish those great things for Him.

Specifically, Jesus said the power would enable them to be effective witnesses for Him. It's worth noting that the leaders in the early church were exceptionally bold and courageous as they lived out the message in front of their friends and neighbors. What is one of the most difficult things to do as a Christian? For many people it's sharing their faith. Many Christians would rather do just about anything except witness to someone about their relationship with Jesus. The baptism with the Holy Spirit will give you a new boldness in life.

5. When you pray in tongues, you are praying with greater effectiveness.

Romans 8:26-27 – *"In the same way, the Spirit helps us in our weakness. We do not know what we ought to pray for, but the Spirit himself intercedes for us with groans that words cannot express. And he who searches our hearts knows the mind of the Spirit, because the Spirit intercedes for the saints in accordance with God's will."*

I Corinthians 14:2 – *"For he who speaks in a tongue does not speak to men*

"When we pray in tongues we're praying or speaking hidden or unrevealed truth."

but to God, for no one understands him; however, in
the spirit he speaks mysteries." (NASB)

Everyone knows the frustration of trying to pray about
a certain situation and not knowing exactly how
to pray. Many times we hesitate, not really asking,
seeking, or knocking for anything in particular because
we're unsure of what God wants or what His will is.
These verses show us that praying in tongues is an
answer to this dilemma. I certainly believe Paul was
referring to praying in the Spirit. It's awesome to know
that as we pray in tongues we're praying in accordance
with God's will!

In the first few verses of I Corinthians 14, Paul is
telling us plainly that when we pray in tongues we're
not speaking to men but to God. How incredible is

that? When I pray in other tongues, I'm praying or speaking straight to God! Then Paul says that in the spirit we speak "mysteries." That's an interesting word for him to use. In our day, in the English language, the word mystery conjures up images of suspense movies, unsolved problems and TV shows. The word in the original language (Greek) literally means hidden or unrevealed truth. I think it's safe to plug that phrase into what is written here. "When we pray in tongues, we're praying or speaking **hidden or unrevealed truth**."

Now that we've looked at the scriptural basis for this gift and experience, let's focus on how to receive it. I encourage you to find a moment when you're in a private, quiet place and you have some time to read through each paragraph. Then, pray the prayer and get ready to receive.

Change Your Mind

The word repent means *to change your mind.* Is there
sin, unforgiveness, pride, fear, doctrinal hang-ups, or
anything in your life blocking you from receiving this
awesome gift? Often believers are simply unaware of
the work of the Holy Spirit. Others have been taught
that this gift is not for them or not for today, or even of
the devil. *Is there anything in your heart or mind that
doesn't line up with God's Word?*

Ask For It

Jesus said in Luke 11:9-13 that all we have to do is
ask and we will receive. Instead of praying, *"Lord, **IF** it
is Your will..."*, start praying, *"Lord, it **IS** Your will..."*
Tell the Lord you want to be baptized with the Holy
Spirit.

Open Your Heart

Reach out by faith and take hold of this gift God freely gives to all who believe in Him. Don't over analyze it with your mind – simply allow your spirit to receive it. Worship the Lord and keep your mind on Him. If someone sends you a gift in the mail, you have to open it to know what it is and to experience the joy that the gift can bring.

Pray Out Loud

The release comes when you stop praying in English (or your native language) and begin praying in tongues. You may at first have only a few words, but go ahead and speak those by faith and others will follow. Often people believe they will be overtaken by God's presence and that God will move their mouths and form the words. But the truth is, *you* have to speak it out! The Bible says that on the Day of Pentecost, the disciples and other believers spoke in tongues as God gave them the ability (Acts 2:4). Don't be afraid to simply speak out. As you do, God will give you the ability to speak in tongues. As you yield yourself, you will begin to sense a wonderful release of worship. Your spirit will overflow with a new sense of the presence of God. You will never be the same!

Remember

The Bible says in John 10:10 that Satan's greatest work is to steal, kill, and destroy. He is called the father of lies and his greatest weapon is to try to confuse you, or cause you to doubt this great gift. Instead, grow in what God has given you and allow your prayer language to develop as you use it in your daily prayer life.

Here is a simple prayer to help you get started. I always encourage people to lift up their hands toward God as a sign of openness, surrender and submission to Him. This is your time. Go for it and get ready to receive.

> "...how much more will your heavenly Father give the Holy Spirit to those who ask him."
>
> Luke 11:13 (NLT)

Father, I come to You in the name of Jesus. I'm hungry for all that You have for me, and I'm seeking with my whole heart to take hold of all that you have for me. Your Word promises that those who hunger will be filled. I believe that it is Your will to give me this great gift of the baptism with the Holy Spirit. Lord, I know this gift is Your will for me, and I have faith right now to receive this gift from You. I know your heart toward me is good and You only want to give me good things, good gifts.

So, I receive it by faith right now. Baptize me and fill me right now with the Holy Spirit. In Jesus' Name, Amen.

The results of a
Spirit-filled life.

THE RESULTS OF A SPIRIT-FILLED LIFE.

Now that we've studied who the Holy Spirit is, and the power of the Holy Spirit in our life, let's finish by looking at some specific results that should be evident in our life if we're filled with the Spirit.

The best place to look is the life of Jesus...

Luke 3:21-22 – *"When all the people were being baptized, Jesus was baptized too. And as he was praying, heaven was opened and the Holy Spirit descended on him in bodily form like a dove. And a voice came from heaven: 'You are my Son, whom I love; with you I am well pleased.'"*

In the Bible, the Jordan River always represents a place of change and transition. For example, when the people crossed from the wilderness into Canaan, they crossed over the Jordan River. There are many other instances, including this one right here in Luke 3 where the Bible tells us that John the Baptist was baptizing people in the Jordan. Jesus was baptized here, too.

When you think about it, there are really two things Jesus did in this story that brought the Holy Spirit into His life. We could call them catalysts - things that initiate the activity of the Holy Spirit in our life. And these same two things are important in our lives as well. Jesus had a spiritual hunger - He wanted to be baptized. Even when John tried to deter Him, Jesus wouldn't have it. He had a hunger for everything his Father had for him, every experience. The first catalyst is hunger. Secondly, this passage says, *"And as he was praying, heaven was opened..."* Prayer is the second catalyst. It brought an open heaven over Jesus' life and when heaven was opened, the Holy Spirit came.

So, Jesus was hungry and He prayed. There is something about these two things that stir up the power of the Holy Spirit in our lives. Hunger put Jesus in the Jordan River and positioned Him for what God wanted to do. Prayer opened heaven and brought the power of the Holy Spirit.

This is pretty awesome. Jesus had an experience with the Holy Spirit. He was filled with the Holy Spirit.

Luke 4:1 – *"Jesus, full of the Holy Spirit, returned from the Jordan..."*

But the best part about it is what happened after Jesus was filled with the Holy Spirit. In Jesus' life there were three specific results of being full of the Holy Spirit. I think we can look at these three things and not only believe for them in our own life, but expect them.

Direction

Luke 4:1 – *"Jesus, full of the Holy Spirit, returned from the Jordan and was led by the Spirit..."*

The first result of a Spirit-filled life is pretty clear and amazing - Jesus was led by the Holy Spirit. I think one of the greatest benefits of Spirit-filled living is that it gives our lives direction.

Throughout the Bible we read promises of God leading and guiding us. All throughout the book of Proverbs there are promises of our steps being ordered by God. In the book of Isaiah it says, *"your ears will hear a voice behind you, saying, 'This is the way; walk in it'"* (Isaiah 30:21). Over and over again we read about the specific promise of direction in the Bible. It's one of the greatest characteristics of the Holy Spirit. The Holy Spirit directs our life.

I know some of you that are reading this right now really need a word from God. You need something from God today. You might have a child in trouble or a marriage that's facing some challenges. Maybe there's a new job opportunity. Whatever it is, if it concerns you, Jesus can and will lead you by the Holy Spirit.

It's definitely one of the results of a life "full of the Spirit" - there will be a sense of direction. We don't need to live in confusion or have a sense of hesitation all the time. We can walk in confidence and boldness, knowing that the Holy Spirit is directing us.

Power

Luke 4:14 – *"Jesus returned to Galilee in the power of the Spirit..."*

The second result of Spirit-filled living is power. Later, Jesus tells His disciples about this characteristic...

Acts 1:8 – *"But you will receive power when the Holy Spirit comes on you; and you will be my witnesses in Jerusalem, and in all Judea and Samaria, and to the ends of the earth."*

The word "power" found in these passages is the Greek word "dunamis" and it's where we get our word dynamite. The power of God is the dynamite in our lives, the power base behind everything we say and do. It's the power of the Holy Spirit that enables us to do three important things – to live out our faith in front of friends and family, to overcome the challenges and problems we're facing and thirdly, to live the full, flourishing life that Jesus promised. When you think about Holy Spirit power working in your life, think about those three things.

Too often as Spirit-filled believers we have focused on the "manifestation" of the Holy Spirit, but really it's about the demonstration. In other words, the effects and results of the Holy Spirit should impact our daily life – not just our Sunday but our Monday, Tuesday,

Wednesday, Thursday, Friday and Saturday. I like to say it this way – the power of God is not only powerful, but also practical.

Purpose

Luke 4:18 – *"The Spirit of the Lord is on me because he has anointed me to..."*

This third result could be an easy one to miss. Just focusing on direction and power are incredible enough, but there has to be a reason for the direction and power beyond just making life better for you. An important word in this famous passage in Luke is the word "because." There is always a "because" when the Holy Spirit is moving in your life.

The word "anointed" here literally means to be covered with the Holy Spirit. Jesus was anointed for a purpose. In fact, this passage clearly says He was anointed to help people; the poor, the prisoners, the blind, and the oppressed.

A clear result of being Spirit-filled is you will be "others" focused. You will be motivated to help other people. This is not only a result, but it's also a good test of your Spirit-filled life. Are you living your life to serve and help other people? The power of the Holy Spirit will enable you to fulfill God's purpose for your life. Ultimately, that purpose will be about helping people. Jesus told His disciples in Acts 1:8 to wait in Jerusalem until the power of the Holy Spirit came into their lives. He explained that the Holy Spirit was coming to give them power to be witnesses for Him.

So, we see that power and purpose work together. There is a purpose for the power and it is to impact other people.

As a Spirit-filled Christian you need to believe God for these three results in your life – direction, power and purpose. Look for them and expect them as you walk out the life God has called you to live.

What is my next step?

That question has become one of the greatest catalysts for personal spiritual growth at our church. So often we're not moving forward because we're overwhelmed with what we want God to do in our lives. Sometimes we can't see the trees for the forest! The thing I've realized is that God just wants us to take that next step that is right before us.

Your next step could be to get planted in a life-giving, Bible-teaching church where you can continue to grow and be encouraged by other believers. If you live in the Memphis, Tennessee area, we'd love to meet you and have you be a part of The Life Church. Visit us online at www.thelifechurch.com for information on service times and locations.

If you live elsewhere, we'd love to help you find a church — just give us a call at 901.751.0095 or check out www.relatedchurches.com to find a church near you.

We've designed the Next Step Series to help people answer the question, "What is my next step?" and to take it. Wherever you are on your journey with God, we hope this series will help strengthen your relationship with God and move you to the next level.

ABOUT THE AUTHOR

John and Leslie Siebeling are the founding pastors of The Life Church based in Memphis, TN. Started in 1996 with just seven people, the church has grown into a thriving, multi-campus church with a diverse congregation numbering in the thousands. John's passion is to see people come to know Jesus and discover the flourishing life God has for them. His gift of teaching the truth of God's Word in a relevant way, transcending cultural, racial and social barriers, has made his weekly television broadcast a success. He is a lead team member for the ARC (Association of Related Churches), an organization that plants new churches throughout the United States. John and Leslie have two children, Anna and Mark. To find out more, visit johnsiebeling.com.